my HORSE HAS Five HeARtS

my HORSE HAS FiVE HeARTS

by KYm & LAken Lee

Written by Kym & Laken Lee
Illustrated by Rusty Fletcher

To my co-author and daughter – you inspire me with your knowledge, compassion and caring each and every day.

KYm

To all of the horses with special hoof care needs.

LAken

My Horse has
five hearts.

One in his
chest . . .

and **FOUR** in his feet!

Does having FIVE hearts
mean he loves me more?

Does he STeP
on his hearts
when he walks
out the door?

No. The heart is wonderful for showing emotion, but it does so much more! It is an important organ that acts like a PUMP.

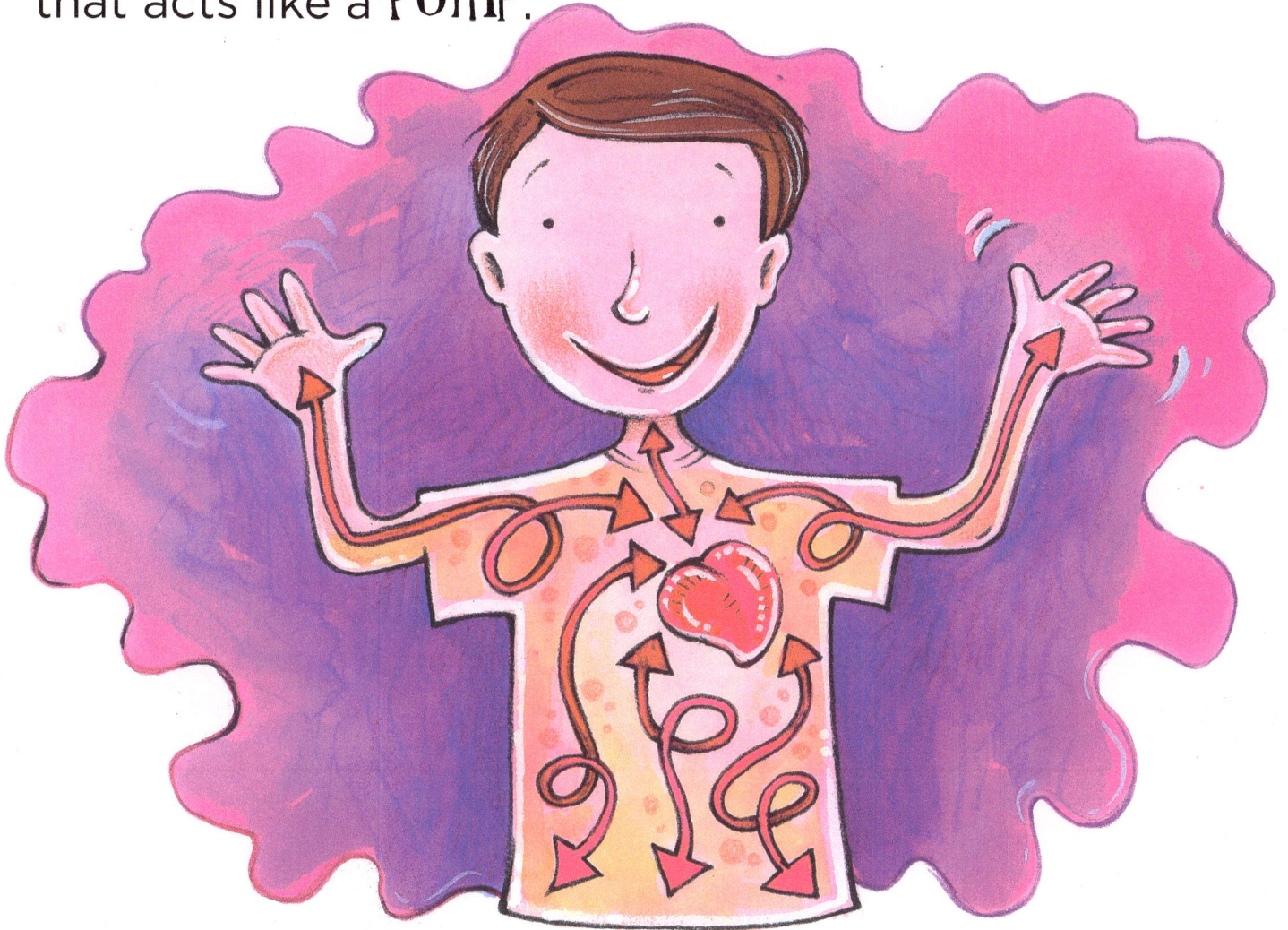

In a person, the heart pushes the blood back and forth and all around the body through a series of arteries with valves.

But in a horse, the valves in his leg only go one way – DOWN!

Luckily the horse's HOOVES force the blood back up the legs, just like four LiTtLe HeARtS!

How do they
do that?

CORONARY
bAND

hOOf WALL

SOLe

fROg

A horse's hoof has a special design. The outside is
made up of a coronary band, hoof wall, sole, and frog.
(No, not thАt kind of frog!)

Inside the hoof is where all the action is happening.

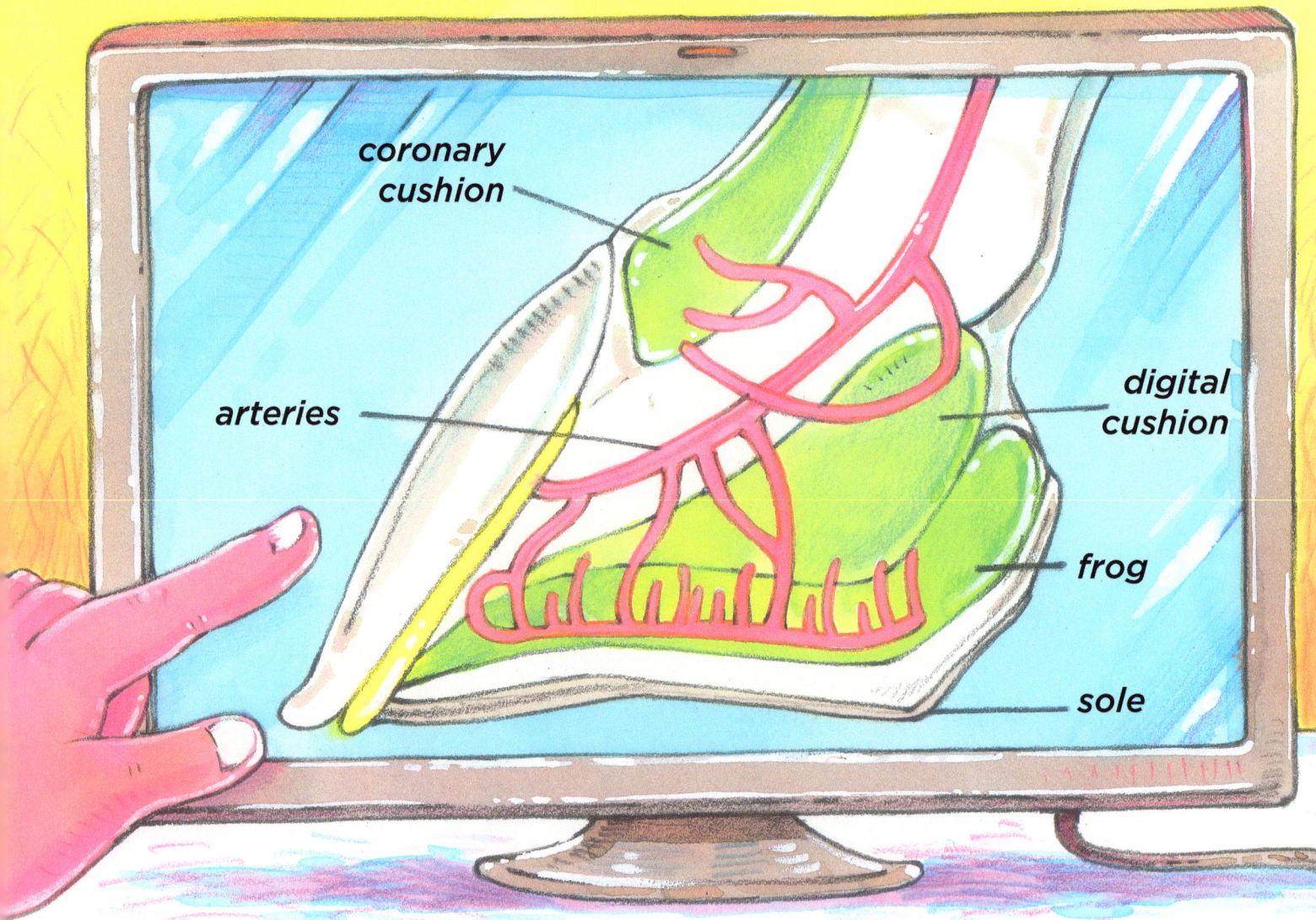

coronary cushion

arteries

digital cushion

frog

sole

A set of ARTeRieS and CUSHionS on the inside combine with the fRog and the SoLe on the outside to create pumping action.

As the horse walks the hooves strike the ground and lift up. This happens over and over again, creating the pump that forces the blood back up the leg.

When the horse trots and canters, this helps the PUMPING action and the blood CIRCULATION even more.

A horse's hooves have to keep their shape to keep the blood circulating all the time.

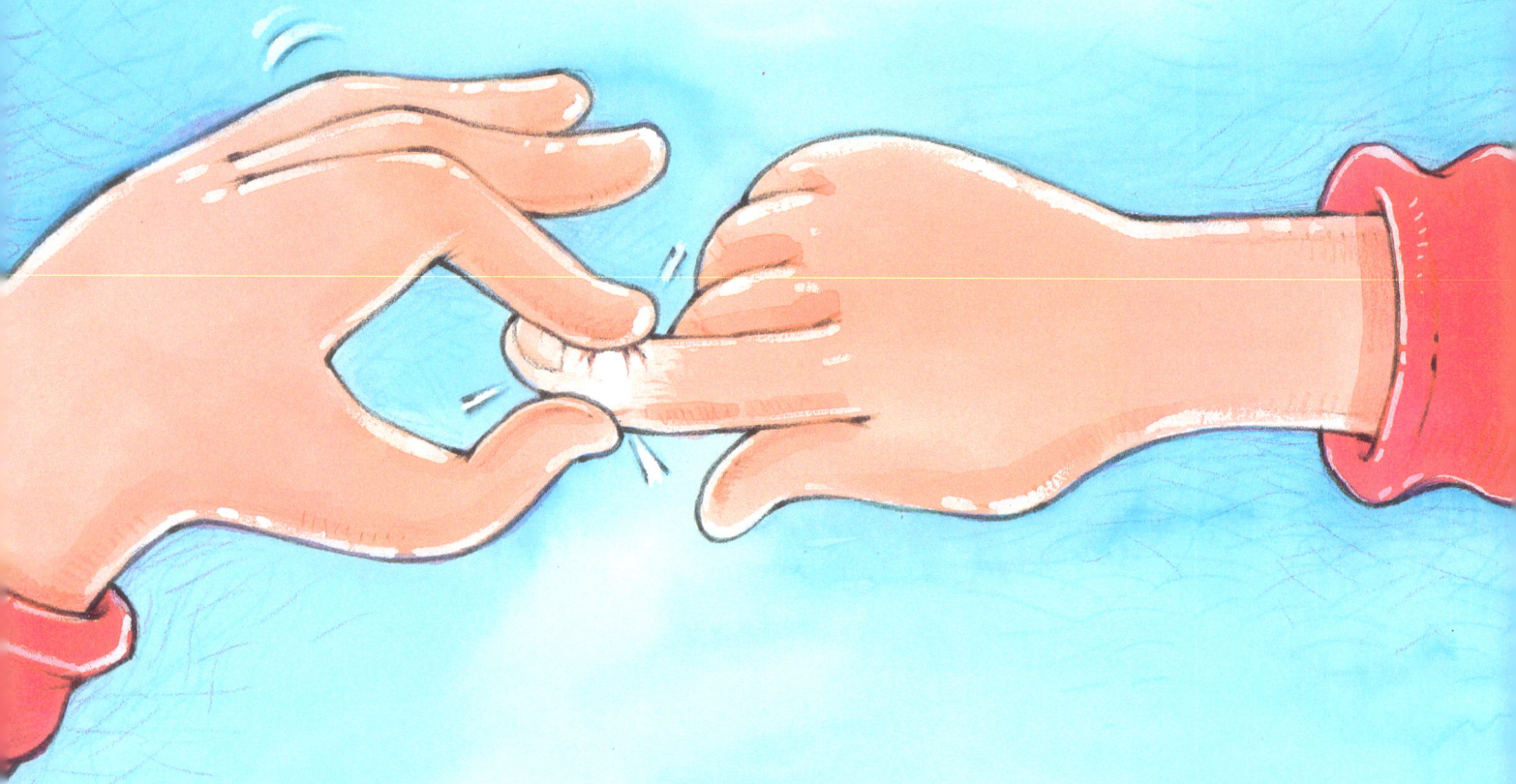

Picture your finger when you SQUEEZE it tight and it turns white. This is from a lack of circulation.

The horse's hoof is like that too.

If the SHAPE of the hoof is not right, those INTERNAL parts get SQUEEZED and circulation cuts off.

HEALTHY HOOF

UNHEALTHY HO

So how do you help the horse take care of all his hearts?

Don't let your horse get too ChUbbY. Extra weight can put pressure on his hooves and they can lose their shape.

Don't let your horse's hooves get too long
and look like pointy slippers.

(SLiPPERS look betteR on genies!)

Don't let the hooves get too wide
and flat so they look like bells.

(BeLLS are betteR for Ringing!)

Hooves should be HEALTHY on the INSIDE and the OUTSIDE to help the horse's body work its best.

Each horse is special in his own way
and the health of all Five hearts is important
no matter what job he is going to do.

Just like we need **EXPERTS** to help us stay **HEALTHY**...

...to be at his best, our HORSES need EXPERTS too.

When you care for
your horse's hooves like hearts,
he will indeed show more love to you.

www.ingramcontent.com/pod-product-compliance
Lightning Source LLC
Chambersburg PA
CBHW041224040426
42443CB00002B/83

* 9 7 8 0 6 1 5 5 6 5 9 7 2 *